HUDSON TALBOTT

RIVER *of* DREAMS

THE STORY OF THE HUDSON RIVER

G. P. PUTNAM'S SONS

*This book is dedicated to Scenic Hudson
in recognition of its leadership in launching the
modern environmental movement and
inspiring citizen activists young and old
to carry on this vital cause.*

When I was growing up in Kentucky, I used to dream about New York, the great city on the river that bore my name—Hudson. It seemed as far away as the Land of Oz, and just as magical and mysterious. At night I would end my prayers with "God bless Mommy and Daddy, may I please have a horse and go to New York? Amen." And then I would drift into dreamland, picturing New York's skyline reaching up to the stars. It was a place of wonder and possibilities. A magnet for dreamers like me.

But the magnet's power actually came from the river. It had been drawing dreamers to it for a *very* long time—long before there was a New York, long before anyone called the river—or me—Hudson.

Thousands of years ago, the glaciers of the last Ice Age carved out the Hudson River valley. When the glaciers melted, the icy water flowed down from the Adirondack Mountains into the river valley where it met the Atlantic Ocean's salt water coming in from the other end. The joining waters created a river that sloshes back and forth as the tides change. The Mahicans called it "Mahekanituck," meaning "the river that flows both ways."

The first people to find their way to the valley were from the great tribal communities of northeastern America. The Mohawks, a tribe of the Iroquois nation, spread through the northern forests and mountains. The Lenni-Lenape, a branch of the Delawares, settled along the shores near the mouth of the river. The valley itself became the land of the Mahicans, an Algonkian-speaking tribe who called themselves the "People of the Great River." For thousands of years the river valley provided all that they needed—food, shelter, transportation, and enough space for everyone.

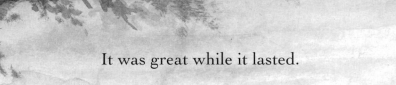

It was great while it lasted.

But other people were dreaming too. . . .

Holland was a tiny nation with very big dreams. It was too small to be a great military power, so instead it turned to trade. The Dutch dreamed of finding a faster route to the riches of China. So they hired one of the greatest dreamers of all time — Henry Hudson.

   Henry was a British explorer who had made two voyages searching for a new route to China. Both trips failed, but they made him famous. When the British fired him, the Dutch asked him to sail for them. In April 1609, Henry set sail from Amsterdam in the *Half Moon*, heading northeast, around Norway. But ice blocked his path, so he turned and headed west, toward the uncharted New World.

New World

Atlantic Ocean

*The land is the finest for cultivation
that I've ever in my life set foot upon.*

— Henry Hudson

The Half Moon crossed the ocean and in September sailed into a great river. Henry hoped he had found the shortcut to China and his path to glory. He explored the river all the way up to present-day Albany before heading home. It was his account of the river, the first written by a European, which brought him lasting fame. But poor Henry never did find China. Two years later his crew mutinied in the icy waters of Canada and set him adrift. He was never seen again.

But the Dutch were on the move. Hearing Henry's tales of the New World, they made ready to stake their claim.

The Dutch set up their first trading post at the tip of Manhattan, an island where the great river meets the Atlantic Ocean and opens into a harbor big enough to hold all the fleets of Europe. Indians soon appeared, loaded down with trade goods. Ships went back to Holland packed with furs and returned to the outpost, now called New Amsterdam, with rowdy adventurers. But the colony was slow to grow because life in Holland was just too comfortable.

So the governors created the *patroon* system. A landowner, or "patroon," would receive huge tracts of land in the river valley, now called New Netherland, in exchange for bringing fifty settlers to work it. By 1650, the colony was booming. But the British became jealous, for their own colonies were failing.

One day in 1664, warships entered the harbor. The captain demanded that the Dutch governor, Peter Stuyvesant, surrender the colony. Tiny Holland had beaten the British Empire at trade, but was no match for their guns. Without a shot fired, the British took the colony and Holland's dream came to an end. But the little trading post begun by the Dutch was on its way to becoming one of the greatest trading centers of all time.

New Amsterdam

Upper Bay

1609
Hudson explores the river

1613
First settlement on Manhattan Island

1624
First families arrive

1626
Peter Minuit pays $24 to Lenape Indians for Manhattan

1647
Peter Stuyvesant arrives as the new lawman in town

1664
New Netherland turned over to the British

Beaver

Amsterdam Coat-of-Arms

Stuyvesant

The British, unlike the Dutch, had plenty of people who wanted to leave England. With high taxes, a harsh class system, and no freedom of religion, many were ready to take their chances in America. But they found the Hudson Valley to be no better. Much of the land was owned by those who had grown rich from the labor of tenant farmers and slaves. The British government forced the colonists to pay taxes in order to finance its vast empire, yet gave them no voice in their own government.

Duke of York

The colony was renamed for the Duke of York, who later became King James II.

1685
Duke of York becomes king, making New York a royal colony

1700s
French and Indian Wars

1765
Riots against the Stamp Act, a new tax

1770
Revolts against British in NY — first blood shed in revolution

1773
Boston Tea Party

1775
Revolutionary War begins

Irish tenant farmer

African slave

LIVINGSTON MANOR

Livingston's tenant farmers

As time passed, the colonists began to think of themselves as American, and anger brewed among rich and poor alike. New dreams began to spread throughout the Hudson Valley, and all of the colonies. Dreams of independence. Dreams of freedom.

King George III

In 1775, *revolution was in the air,* and the British were ready with a brilliant strategy. By taking control of the Hudson River they would cut New England off from the other colonies and crush the revolution before it started. The plan was to attack from the north and south and meet in the middle. They took New York City, giving them a base for moving upriver. But their march southward from Canada was stopped at the Battle of Saratoga, the first great American victory in the war. Hearing of the defeat, the British in the lower Hudson went on a rampage, attacking river towns, and finally burning Kingston, New York's capital at that time. The valley was now an open and dangerous battleground.

July, 1776
Declaration
of Independence

July, 1776
Only naval battle
on Hudson,
at Tappan Zee

Sept., 1776
Congress changes name
from United Colonies
to United States

Nov., 1776
New York City
falls to British

June, 1777
British invade NY
from Canada to take
Hudson Valley from north

July, 1777
Ticonderoga,
Ft. Ann, Ft. Edward
fall to British

West Point

When George Washington made his headquarters on a steep cliff overlooking the river, it became the most important military post in the country. Known as West Point, it had views of all boat traffic in both directions. The river wrapped around its base, forcing ships to slow down and to come into easy range of cannon fire. Washington called West Point the "key to America."

Benedict Arnold

A courageous army officer, Arnold was the hero of the Battle of Saratoga. When he didn't receive the glory he felt was due him, he grew angry and bitter. After becoming the chief officer of West Point, he secretly passed the plans of its defenses to a British spy. The spy was caught, but Benedict escaped to England. He has been a symbol of betrayal ever since.

WEST POINT

Benedict Arnold

Chaining the Hudson

Called "Washington's watch fob," a massive chain made of huge iron links was floated across the river on a bed of logs at West Point. Although never challenged, it was enough to discourage the British. They soon gave up on capturing the Hudson and moved the fighting to Virginia, where they were finally defeated.

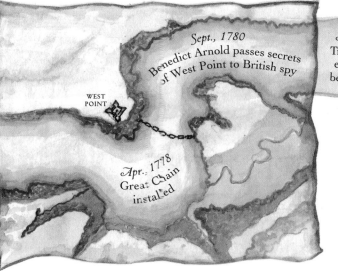

Oct., 1777
Ft. Montgomery,
Ft. Clinton
fall to British

Oct., 1777
Battle of Saratoga
changes tide of war

Oct., 1777
British burn
Kingston

Sept., 1780
Benedict Arnold passes secrets
of West Point to British spy

April, 1783
Treaty of Paris
ends war; U.S.
begins as a nation

WEST POINT

Apr., 1778
Great Chain
installed

Fighting together had united Americans, and now they joined together in work, sharing a vision for their young land. It was a new nation with a new dream, and the Hudson sparkled with new energy.

sloop

Boats of all shapes and sizes were seen on the river but the real workhorse was the Hudson River sloop. Based on the old Dutch sloop, it was shallow enough to avoid the rocks, but wide enough for ample cargo or passengers. It dominated river trade for over two centuries.

bark

schooner

Even whaling ships appeared on the Hudson, when two brothers came from Nantucket in search of a safer home for their whaling fleet. They found a small port and renamed it Hudson. The little boomtown soon harbored dozens of whalers and other merchant ships, which traveled all over the world. By 1820, Hudson was second only to New York City in volume of shipping trade.

In the early 1800s, two events occurred in the valley which changed the course of world history and made the Hudson River the most important inland trade route.

Fulton's Steamboat

The Clermont

"Teakettle on a Raft"

Fulton's Steamboat

Robert Fulton did not invent the steamboat, but he was the first to make it commercially useful when he launched the *Clermont* in 1807. The great advantage of steam was not speed, but reliability. No one had to wait for a "good wind" anymore. Regularly scheduled trips made business boom and opened the river up to hundreds of sightseers. Fulton's dream made him rich. But the wealth that would flow from the river was just beginning.

QUEEN OF THE CATSKILLS

1807   1825   1850   1875

The Erie Canal

George Washington had once envisioned a canal across New York State, connecting the waters of Lake Erie to the Hudson. Governor Dewitt Clinton picked up the dream, and finally saw it completed in 1825. Three hundred and sixty-three miles long, forty feet wide and only four feet deep, its nickname switched overnight from "Clinton's Ditch" to the "Eighth Wonder of the World."

The Erie Canal

The Seneca Chief

"Clinton's Ditch"

Hudson River

Suddenly, the great, untapped heartland of America was connected to the world by water. New York-to-Cleveland travel time went from ninety days by land to thirty days by water. The price of grain dropped from ninety cents a pound to nine cents as Midwestern farm products flooded eastward. Flooding westward were immigrants, eager to stake a claim in the rich Midwestern farmland. Any town linked to the Erie system leaped in prosperity, but none more so than New York City, which would become America's largest seaport.

Albany

Buffalo

New York City

Midwest

Lake Erie

Boats were pulled by horses or mules and went 1½ miles per hour.

Passengers paid 1½ cents per mile.

Boats passed through 83 locks because Buffalo is 568 ft. higher than Albany.

New York State paid for the canal. It recouped the cost within seven years.

During the opening ceremonies for the Erie Canal, Governor Clinton poured a keg of water from Lake Erie into New York Harbor in a symbolic "wedding of the waters," binding the Great Lakes to the Atlantic Ocean.

The Hudson became America's first superhighway, and it made New York City into the greatest marketplace on earth. Money was pouring into the city from all directions.

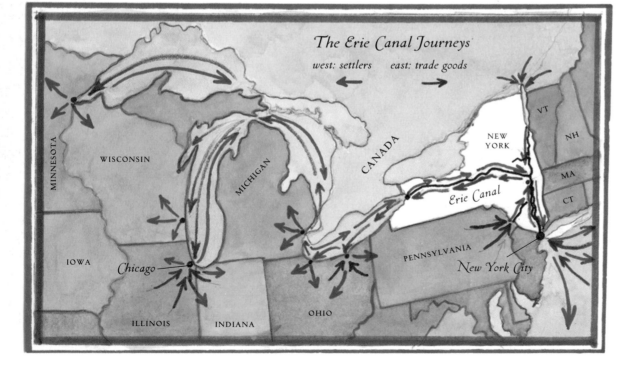

The Erie Canal Journeys

west: settlers   east: trade goods

←   →

Soon, more canals were added, bringing the products of Canadian forests and the Pennsylvania coalfields to the stream coming down the Hudson.

The financial and
banking business sprang up
along a street where the wall of the old
Dutch village once stood. Named Wall Street,
it has remained the center of world
finance ever since.

Wall Street

Winter froze the Hudson River solid, stopping the boat traffic for several months, but even that couldn't slow the growth of industry in the Hudson Valley. Harvesting the ice became a big business, employing thousands of farmers and others needing work in the wintertime. When the river thawed, boats carried the ice as far away as India. But most of the ice was destined for the iceboxes in the rapidly growing city of New York.

Iceboating became a favorite sport. People sailed far faster on ice than they could on water.

Ferry sleighs took passengers across the river in deep winter.

For ice harvesting, a grid was cut by horses pulling saw blades. Then blocks of ice weighing about 300 pounds were put on a conveyor belt leading to an icehouse to await shipment. It was great business, for the ice was free—a gift of the river.

The Hudson River valley had been a center of commercial activity for two centuries, but now it was becoming a source of inspiration for the writers who lived there. They began creating a literature that Americans could call their own.

Washington Irving of Tarrytown was the first American to fully support himself by his work as a writer. Famous for his tales of the early Dutch settlers, such as the story of Ichabod Crane and the Headless Horseman, he truly captured the American imagination with his tale of Rip Van Winkle, a young colonist who falls asleep for twenty years while hiking in the Catskills. He awakens to find that he's now an old man in a new nation. Perhaps many readers felt that way as life around them was changing so rapidly in the new century.

His friend James Fenimore Cooper wrote dramatic tales of frontier life in colonial America. His *Last of the Mohicans*, set in the northern Hudson region, portrayed Indians as either noble or savage, and colonial Americans as rugged pioneers, pushing back the wilderness yet loving nature. They are themes that have run through American literature ever since, and continue to influence the way we think of ourselves as Americans.

In 1825, a young artist named *Thomas Cole* traveled
up the Hudson, drawn by its unspoiled beauty. Deeply motivated by his
faith, he saw Nature as the perfect expression of God's own artwork. Although
he painted many scenes from the Bible, it was his breathtaking paintings of the
Catskill Mountains and Hudson Valley which struck a chord with the public.

For the first time, Americans could look with pride at the grandeur of their own land, the land they loved and fought for, and which now was giving them so much in return.

Cole was joined by his friend Asher Durand, and then by Frederick Church, who became his student. By the time of Cole's death in 1848, landscape painters from all over America were flocking to the Hudson Valley, and the first American-based art movement was born. It was known as the Hudson River School of painting, and it dominated American art for the rest of the century.

But the landscape was about to change. . . .

The Industrial Revolution now swept through the nation, carried by an "Iron Horse."

The coming of the railroads was perhaps the single most dramatic change in nineteenth-century America. The freight train quickly overtook the Erie Canal as the driving force of industry, carrying it faster and farther across the ever-expanding nation. New York City prospered even more, as the fortunes made from the canal were now being invested in a vast network of railroad empires. By 1869, trains linked the entire country, delivering goods, mail and passengers from coast to coast.

For New York City and the Hudson Valley,
it was full steam ahead. . . .

By the 1880s, it seemed that all railroads led to New York City. With its rise to power as America's most important port and the center of world trade came the ever-increasing need for speed in moving products and people. The railroad companies needed flat land for laying down tracks, and found it along the banks of the Hudson. Factories sprang up along the train lines, making it faster and easier to ship their goods.

With all the money pouring into the city the era came to be known as the Gilded Age. The rich built mansions overlooking the river, and some had their own train stops.

The Hudson was busier than ever, but it would never be the same. The train tracks bound up the river's shoreline, slicing through bays and inlets. No one was allowed to cross the tracks, making it nearly impossible to reach the river anymore.

But the focus had shifted from the river to the railroad. In 1888 the first bridge to span the Hudson opened at Poughkeepsie, and it was for trains.

There was now another river flowing into New York Harbor from the other side of the ocean—a river of dreamers. From all over the world, they came to try their luck in the land of opportunity, bringing with them a few bags and their own version of the American Dream. But what started as a trickle of dreamers became a flood by the century's end. In less than a hundred years, New York City's population rapidly multiplied to over a million and a half people! To process the masses of immigrants a station was opened on Ellis Island, where papers were checked and medical exams given before the newcomers could enter the country.

On the way to Ellis Island, they passed a sight which reminded them of what they were all seeking: liberty.

Standing at the front door of America, the Statue of Liberty has welcomed millions ever since she herself arrived in 1886, a gift from the people of France. A verse from the poem on her base speaks for her:

Give me your tired, your poor,
Your huddled masses yearning to breathe free,
The wretched refuse from your teeming shore.
Send these, the tempest-tost to me,
I lift my lamp beside the golden door!

— *Emma Lazarus*

By the twentieth century, New York City had long since reached its destiny of becoming the most powerful city in America. In less than 300 years it had grown from a tiny Dutch outpost in the wilderness to the business capital of the world. It was a city built on dreams.

But it was made out of bricks and cement that had come from the banks of the Hudson. The river which had fed all those dreams was now fading into the background. New York didn't seem to need the river anymore, except as a

Industry on the river had made some New Yorkers filthy rich. But it just made the river filthy. Garbage, factory waste, plant chemicals and the raw sewage of the cities and towns along its banks were dumped directly into the river. The water turned greenish brown, except by the GM plant, where it turned red or yellow or whatever color that they were painting the cars that day.

The fishing industry collapsed. The few fish that survived were too poisonous to eat. Smog from the factory smoke and dust from the cement plants blanketed the valley. And it was all legal.

Most people don't start out with dreams of polluting a river. But it was often the result of people chasing their dreams of wealth with little care of how they reached it. The Hudson Valley had always drawn them.

But now there were other dreamers in the valley, with their own dreams of wealth. They dreamed of the wealth of wildlife in a healthy forest, the abundance of fish in oxygen-rich water, and the great fortune of living in a beautiful river valley.

So perhaps it was a matter of time before the two types of dreamers would meet each other—in court.

PROPOSED PLANT

In 1963 Con Edison,
New York City's power company,
proposed a plan for constructing the largest
hydroelectric pumping station ever built. The plan
called for carving out a gigantic hole in the side of majestic
Storm King Mountain on the Hudson River.

But then they met Franny Reese. Franny was a longtime valley resident with a simple point to make: The mountain could not speak for itself. If she didn't speak for it, who would?

Franny and a group of like-minded people founded Scenic Hudson and took on the power company in a landmark court case. Con Ed challenged the right of private citizens to participate, but the court sided with the citizens, in a ruling now known as the Scenic Hudson Decision.

After dragging out the case for seventeen years, Con Ed finally gave up and Storm King survived unblemished. It was the beginning of the environmental movement in this country, and once again, the Hudson Valley was the birthplace.

More and more people joined the movement as they realized how much difference each of us can make.

Franny Reese

Pete Seeger

Clearwater

1969
Hudson River Sloop *Clearwater* launched by legendary folksinger Pete Seeger as a tool for educating the public about being caretakers of the environment

1965
Scenic Hudson Decision launches the environmental movement

The love of their land was still alive in the hearts of Americans, and now that it was aroused again, things began to change.

Many new laws and new citizens' groups have been inspired by those early heroes of the environment, and their work has begun to bring the Hudson River back to life.

The Mahicans called it "The River That Flows Both Ways." Slowly we are learning that taking care of the river is the only way that the river can take care of us.

Hudson shad

1978
Endangered Species Act
passed

1972
National Environmental
Policy Act passed

1963
Clean Air Act
passed

1970
Environmental Protection
Agency formed

1972
Clean Water Act
passed

osprey

Hudson Shad
Once a major commercial fish, the shad are slowly making a comeback. They swim upriver to spawn every spring, when the shadblow tree blooms.

Osprey
Called the "fish hawk," the osprey was almost wiped out by the chemical DDT, which was banned in 1972. Ospreys now return every spring, following the spawning shad.

Striped Bass

The number-one sport fish, they are returning in larger numbers, but commercial fishing has not yet been authorized. The record striper was caught in 2007: 55 lbs. 7 oz.

bald eagle

Bald Eagle

Gone from the valley for over a hundred years, eagles were sighted once again in 1992. There are now believed to be over 300 nesting pairs in the valley.

1990s
Swimming returns to the Hudson River

1983
Hudson Riverkeeper, Inc. formed. Citizens watchdog group catches and prosecutes polluters and safeguards the river

1991
Hudson Valley Greenway formed. Created to develop both sides of river into green, eco-friendly recreational areas, from Albany to New York City

1996
Hudson River Valley National Heritage Area established by Congress to preserve the cultural and natural resources of the area for the benefit of the nation

striped bass

Atlantic Sturgeon

The "king of freshwater fishes" were once so common they were nicknamed "Albany beef," and their eggs, called caviar, were in great demand. After becoming endangered, they are now protected and slowly making a comeback.

Atlantic sturgeon

Fifty years have passed since I dreamed of going to New York to see the river that shares my name, and thirty-five years since that dream came true. I live in the Hudson Valley now, grateful to all those who came before me, following their dreams to this river, building this nation, sharing its beauty, securing its future.

It's now my turn to help in keeping the river of dreams flowing,
for all those dreamers yet to come.

"I thank God I was born on the banks of the Hudson! . . .
We make a friendship with it, we in a manner ally ourselves to it for life.
It remains an object of our pride and affections, a rallying point,
to call us home again after all our wanderings."

—Washington Irving

For further reading:

Boyle, Robert. *The Hudson River: A Natural and Unnatural History.* New York: W. W. Norton & Company, 1979.

Carmer, Carl. *The Hudson.* New York: Grosset & Dunlap, 1968.

Cronin, John, and Robert F. Kennedy Jr. *The Riverkeepers: Two Activists Fight to Reclaim Our Environment as a Basic Human Right.* New York: Scribner, 1997.

Komroff, Manuel. *The Hudson: From Lake Tear of the Clouds to New York Harbor.* New York: McGraw-Hill, 1969.

Lewis, Tom. *The Hudson: A History.* New Haven, Conn.: Yale University Press, 2005.

Lossing, Benson J. *The Hudson: From the Wilderness to the Sea.* Hensonville, N.Y.: Black Dome Press, 2000.

Mylod, John. *Biography of a River: The People and Legends of the Hudson Valley.* New York: Bonanza Books, 1978.

Shorto, Russell. *The Island at the Center of the World: The Epic Story of Dutch Manhattan and the Forgotten Colony That Shaped America.* New York: Doubleday, 2004.

Stanne, Stephen P., Roger G. Panetta, and Brian E. Forist. *The Hudson: An Illustrated Guide to the Living River.* New Brunswick, N.J.: Rivergate Books, 2007.

Van Zandt, Roland. *The Catskill Mountain House.* Hensonville, N.Y.: Black Dome Press, 1997.

Websites:

Scenic Hudson **www.scenichudson.org** Works to protect and restore the majestic landscape of the Hudson River Valley

The Thomas Cole National Historic Site **www.thomascole.org** Home of Thomas Cole, founder of the Hudson River School of painting

Clearwater **www.clearwater.org** Operates the Hudson River sloop, which conducts environmental education

Riverkeeper **www.riverkeeper.org** An environmental "neighborhood watch" group dedicated to guarding the nation's waters

The New Netherland Museum **www.newnetherland.org** Operates the replica ship *Half Moon* on the Hudson River

G. P. PUTNAM'S SONS
A division of Penguin Young Readers Group. Published by The Penguin Group. Penguin Group (USA) Inc., 375 Hudson Street, New York, NY 10014, U.S.A.
Penguin Group (Canada), 90 Eglinton Avenue East, Suite 700, Toronto, Ontario M4P 2Y3, Canada (a division of Pearson Penguin Canada Inc.). Penguin Books Ltd, 80 Strand, London WC2R 0RL, England. Penguin Ireland, 25 St. Stephen's Green, Dublin 2, Ireland (a division of Penguin Books Ltd.). Penguin Group (Australia), 250 Camberwell Road, Camberwell, Victoria 3124, Australia (a division of Pearson Australia Group Pty Ltd). Penguin Books India Pvt Ltd, 11 Community Centre, Panchsheel Park, New Delhi - 110 017, India. Penguin Group (NZ), 67 Apollo Drive, Rosedale, North Shore 0632, New Zealand (a division of Pearson New Zealand Ltd). Penguin Books (South Africa) (Pty) Ltd, 24 Sturdee Avenue, Rosebank, Johannesburg 2196, South Africa. Penguin Books Ltd, Registered Offices: 80 Strand, London WC2R 0RL, England.

Library of Congress Cataloging-in-Publication Data
Talbott, Hudson. River of dreams : the story of the Hudson River / Hudson Talbott.   p. cm.   1. Hudson River (N.Y. and N.J.)—History—Juvenile literature.
2. Hudson River Valley (N.Y. and N.J.)—History—Juvenile literature. I. Title.   F127.H8T23 2009   974.7'3—dc22   2008018581   ISBN 978-0-399-24521-3

10 9 8 7 6 5 4 3 2 1